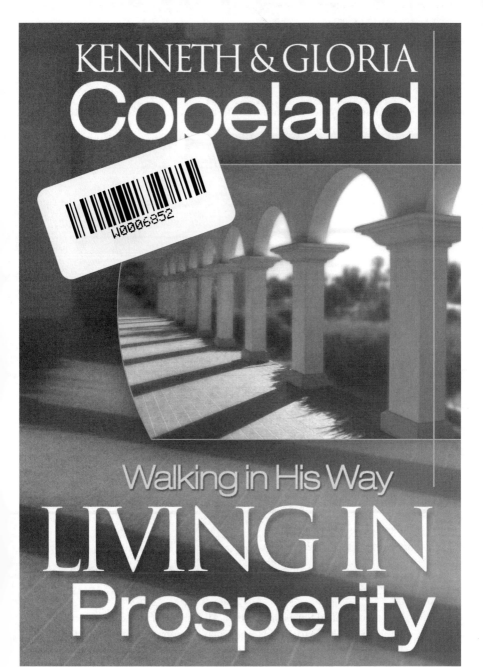

KENNETH & GLORIA
Copeland

W0006852

Walking in His Way
LIVING IN
Prosperity

JESUS IS LORD

KENNETH

COPELAND

PUBLICATIONS

Unless otherwise noted, all scripture is from the *King James Version* of the Bible.

Scripture quotations marked *The Amplified Bible* are from *The Amplified Bible, Old Testament* © 1965, 1987 by the Zondervan Corporation. *The Amplified New Testament* © 1958, 1987 by The Lockman Foundation. Used by permission.

Living in Prosperity

ISBN-10   1-57562-735-3   30-0734
ISBN-13   978-1-57562-735-9

19 18 17 16 15 14   11 10 9 8 7 6

Kenneth Copeland Publications
Fort Worth, TX 76192-0001

For more information about Kenneth Copeland Ministries, visit kcm.org or call 1-800-600-7395 (U.S. only) or +1-817-852-6000.

1

"Beloved, I wish above all things that thou mayest prosper and be in health, even as thy soul prospereth."

3 John 2

CD ONE

Laws That Govern Prosperity

The Law of Giving
Is the Very Life and
Heart of God

The Yardstick of Prosperity

God's will for mankind is prosperity. In his third epistle, John states, "Beloved, I wish above all things that thou mayest prosper and be in health, even as thy soul prospereth" (verse 2). He goes on to say that he has no greater joy than to hear that his children (spiritual offspring) walk in the truth. The truth of The Word of God is that He desires for believers to be prosperous.

The world defines prosperity as financial, political and military power. It is based on a scale of dollars and cents. But true prosperity is the ability to use God's ability and power to meet any need in any realm of mankind's existence: spirit, soul, body, financially and socially.

> *A law will work every time it is put to work.*

Every realm of prosperity is governed by laws. God's Word is law. A law will work every time it is put to work. For example, there is a law concerning salvation. It is found in Romans 10:9-10: *Confess* with the mouth the Lord Jesus and *believe* in the heart that God has raised Him from the dead. When a man acts on that law, the result will be that he experiences the new birth.

Love is the cardinal law of the realm of the spirit. How does the law of love affect the laws of prosperity? To love is to give. God is a giver and those who are born of Him manifest His love as they give. This applies to every realm. Giving is interwoven into everything God does.

"For God so loved the world, that he gave his only begotten

Son, that whosoever believeth in him should not perish, but have everlasting life" (John 3:16). God gave His only Son and He continues to receive sons. Jesus gave His life of His own free will. Now, as born-again believers, we can be vessels through which He gives His life to others. His life continues to be reproduced every time a man receives Him as Lord and becomes born again.

> *Spiritual prosperity is to have the life of God residing in your spirit man.*

Spiritual prosperity is to have the life of God residing in your spirit man. It is realizing your place in Christ Jesus and learning what your rights and privileges are as a new creation.

Mental prosperity is having The Word of God dominating your thought life. Peace comes from knowing what The Word says. You exercise that peace which passes all understanding. You recognize the fact that the Greater One dwelling in you is more than able to handle problems, situations and circumstances you face.

Physical prosperity is twofold. It is health and financial wealth. As you have received healing by the redemptive work of Jesus, it is your place to lay your hands on the sick and they will recover. In Acts 3, Peter said to the lame man that he did not have silver and gold to give him, but he knew the power in the Name of Jesus. He knew that through faith in that Name the man would be made whole—and he was (Acts 3:2-8, 16). ✑

Whatever your situation, in any realm of life, God is able to handle it. He is willing to use His ability and His power on your behalf so that all of your needs are met.

ℭ𝒟 *1* 𝒪*utlined*

I. Prosperity is God's will (3 John 2)

II. World's definition of prosperity

III. Definition of true prosperity

IV. Prosperity is governed by laws
   A. Will work when put to work

V. Cardinal law of God is love
   A. Love gives
      1. Must give to be prosperous

VI. Spiritual prosperity is to be born again

VII. Mental prosperity is peace

VIII. Physical prosperity is twofold
   A. Healing
   B. Wealth

Study Questions

(1) How do we know that prosperity is God's will? _____

_____

_____

_____

_____

(2) Give the definition of true prosperity. _____

_____

_____

_____

(3) How does the cardinal law of love affect the laws of prosperity?

_____

_____

_____

_____

(4) What is spiritual prosperity? _____

_____

_____

_____

_____

(5) What is mental prosperity? _____

_____

_____

_____

_____

Study Notes

"But whoso looketh into the perfect law of liberty,
and continueth therein...this man shall be blessed in his deed."
James 1:25

2

"For I rejoiced greatly,
when the brethren came
and testified of The
[Word] that is in thee,
even as thou walkest in
The [Word]. I have no
greater joy than to hear
that my children walk
in [The Word]."

3 John 3-4 *author's paraphrase*

CD TWO
Laws That Govern Giving

Jesus Has Provided the Tools to Put the Law of Prosperity Into Motion—His Word and His Name

Prosperity Was Bought at Calvary

The law of giving is the primary law. We see it in action in the area of planting seed. Give one seed and it will produce more seeds. A kernel of corn gives itself to produce a whole ear of corn—first the blade, then the ear, then the full corn in the ear. Then when the grain is ripe the sickle is put in, for the harvest is ready.

Prosperity covers every realm of life, not just finances. It is not how much money a man has but how he handles what he does have. The Bible says God gives us all things richly but we are to see to it that we do our part in distributing it. It is God who has given us the power to get wealth. It is God who has the ability to show us how to handle it correctly.

> *Prosperity covers every realm of life, not just finances.*

Jesus was anointed to preach prosperity in every realm of human existence. "The Spirit of the Lord is upon me, because he hath anointed me to preach the gospel to the poor; he hath sent me to heal the brokenhearted, to preach deliverance to the captives, and recovering of sight to the blind, to set at liberty them that are bruised, to preach the acceptable year of the Lord" (Luke 4:18-19).

The acceptable year of the Lord was the year of Jubilee. Every 50th year was set aside to let the land rest from planting, to return property to the original owner, to allow slaves to be set free and debts to be canceled. It was a time of refreshing and a new start in life. In the 49th year, God increased their crops so they would have enough to sustain them for three years (that year, the 50th year when they could not plant and the 51st year while they were waiting for the harvest).

Jesus was saying, "The Jubilee is a person and I am He." Jesus is the fulfillment of total prosperity. He released all of mankind from spiritual, mental, physical, financial and social bankruptcy.

God is able to make every favor and earthly blessing come to you in abundance so you will possess enough to require no aid or support and enough to give (2 Corinthians 9:8, *The Amplified Bible*).

Love is the basis for giving.

Love is the basis for giving. In Luke 6, Jesus said to love your enemies, to do good to those who hate you, to bless those who curse you and to pray for those who despitefully use you (verses 27-28). Verse 35 says to love your enemies and do good and lend, hoping for nothing again. This does not mean to hope for nothing from God, but to hope for nothing from the one to whom you made the loan. Verse 38 says, "Give, and it shall be given unto you.... For with the same measure that ye mete withal it shall be measured to you again." This giving must be done from the standpoint of love and not with the idea of giving in order to get.

The Apostle Paul wrote, "And though I bestow all my goods to feed the poor, and though I give my body to be burned, and have not charity [the God kind of love], it profiteth me nothing" (1 Corinthians 13:3). Commit to love and you will be a giver. Then receive the blessings of God by faith.

CD 2 Outlined

I. Law of giving is the primary law
   A. Plant one seed and it will produce more seeds

II. Kingdom of God compared to planting seed

III. The *love* of money, not money, is the root of all evil

IV. Jesus preached prosperity in every realm of human existence
   A. It is available to Him, the fulfillment of total prosperity
   B. He is the Jubilee (acceptable year of the Lord)

V. God blesses us so we can distribute to others

VI. Love is the basis for giving (Luke 6:27-38)
   A. Without love, giving profits you nothing

Study Questions

(1) Why is giving the primary law? _____

_____

_____

_____

_____

(2) According to 1 Timothy 6, why does God give to the believer richly?

_____

_____

_____

_____

(3) Why is the acceptable year of the Lord—the Jubilee—a person?

_____

_____

_____

_____

(4) What is the basis for giving? _____

_____

_____

(5) What must we do to receive the blessings of God? _____

_____

_____

_____

_____

Study Notes

"But seek ye first the kingdom of God, and his righteousness;
and all these things shall be added unto you."
Matthew 6:33

3

"And God is able to make all grace (every favor and earthly blessing) come to you in abundance, so that you may always and under all circumstances and whatever the need be self-sufficient [possessing enough to require no aid or support and furnished in abundance for every good work and charitable donation]."

2 Corinthians 9:8, *The Amplified Bible*

CD THREE
Prosperity Is Ours

Everything It Takes for You to Be a Success Was Bought and Paid for at Calvary

Our Covenant Lacks Nothing

Adam was created to live in total prosperity: spirit, soul and body. When he committed high treason, Satan was given authority and a curse came upon all men. Mankind was in need of a way out of the curse and God needed legal entry back into the earth.

God found a man who would, by faith, make covenant with Him. He changed his name from Abram to Abraham, meaning a father of many nations. This meant that all those who were the seed of Abraham were entitled to live under the covenant God made with him. This covenant, as all other covenants, had blessings and cursings. In this way, God could provide a way for man to receive His blessings and have an umbrella of protection from the curses that already existed because of Adam's transgression.

The blessings are guaranteed *if* a man harkens diligently unto the voice of the Lord God to observe and to do all His commandments (Deuteronomy 28:1). The first 14 verses of Deuteronomy 28 list the blessings. They include everything necessary to live a prosperous life. "And the Lord shall make thee plenteous in goods, in the fruit of thy body, and in the fruit of thy cattle, and in the fruit of thy ground…and thou shalt lend unto many nations, and thou shalt not borrow. And the Lord shall make thee the head, and not the tail; and thou shalt be above only, and thou shalt not be beneath" (Deuteronomy 28:11-13). God said He would

> *The blessings are guaranteed if a man harkens diligently unto the voice of the Lord God.*

command the blessings upon all that they set their hand to (Deuteronomy 28:8).

Poverty is not a blessing. It is a curse. "Thou shalt carry much seed out into the field, and shalt gather but little in.... Thou shalt plant vineyards, and dress them, but shalt neither drink of the wine, nor gather the grapes.... The stranger that is within thee shall get up above thee very high; and thou shalt come down very low. He shall lend to thee, and thou shalt not lend to him: he shall be the head, and thou shalt be the tail" (Deuteronomy 28:38-39, 43-44).

The covenant and its blessings were a picture of Jesus. He was the fulfillment of prosperity in every realm: spirit, soul, body, financially and socially. He "redeemed us from the curse of the law, being made a curse for us" so the blessings might come on the Gentiles through Him (Galatians 3:13-14).

When Jesus was raised from the dead, everyone who would accept His substitutionary sacrifice became a seed of Abraham. "And if ye be Christ's, then are ye Abraham's seed, and heirs according to the promise" (Galatians 3:29). "For the promise, that he should be the heir of the world, was not to Abraham, or to his seed, through the law, but through the righteousness of faith" (Romans 4:13).

In the mind of God, every believer is whole and sound in his body and lacks no good thing. The power of the law of sin and death that contained the curse was broken forever. Jesus stripped Satan and left him with nothing, giving back to us all that had been lost by Adam. ❧

> *The covenant and its blessings were a picture of Jesus.*

The Cross was for us, not God.
He was not in need of prosperity
and health. He was not in need of
redemption. But He met our needs
in Christ Jesus and redemption was
a complete work. Jesus paid it all so
we could live in Him and walk free
of the law of sin and death and all
the curse of the law. God wants us
to live the abundant life. Blessing
us is His good pleasure.

C D 3 O u t l i n e d

I. Man was created to live in total prosperity:
   A. Spirit
   B. Soul
   C. Body

II. Adam's high treason gave Satan authority and a curse came upon all men

III. God made a covenant with man
   A. It provided protection
   B. It provided blessings
      1. Blessings were contingent upon:
         a. Harkening diligently to the voice of God
         b. Observing and doing *all* commandments

IV. Poverty is a curse

V. Jesus redeemed us from the curse of the law so Abraham's blessings could be ours

VI. God sees us complete in Jesus

Study Questions

1) How do we know it is God's perfect will for man to live in total prosperity? _____

_____

_____

_____

(2) Explain the benefits of the old covenant. _____

_____

_____

_____

(3) Why are believers today entitled to the blessings of Abraham?

_____

_____

_____

_____

(4) How does God see the believer and why? _____

_____

_____

_____

(5) Why is it important for us to harken diligently unto the voice of the Lord and obey His Word? _____

_____

_____

_____

Study Notes

"For the law of the Spirit of life in Christ Jesus
hath made me free from the law of sin and death."
Romans 8:2

4

"*For this cause we also, since the day we heard it, do not cease to pray for you, and to desire that ye might be filled with the knowledge of his will in all wisdom and spiritual understanding.*"

Colossians 1:9

CD FOUR

Drawing Wisdom for Prosperity

All the Treasures of Wisdom and Knowledge Are Hidden in Jesus—And He's in You!

Apply Your Heart to God's Word—Do It by Faith

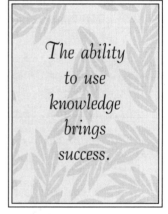

The ability to use knowledge brings success.

The ability to use knowledge brings success. Wisdom is the ability to use knowledge. Jesus said, in Luke 11:49, that the wisdom of God is The Word of God. Therefore, total prosperity for every area of a man's life is found in The Word.

Jesus came to preach the gospel to the poor. God wanted the people to know they did not need to be poor anymore. Jesus came to tell the brokenhearted they did not have to be brokenhearted any longer. He came to set the captives free. God's desire is for every man to be free—spirit, soul, body, financially and socially.

In the book of Proverbs, Solomon wrote this about wisdom:

> Happy is the man that findeth wisdom, and the man that getteth understanding. For the merchandise of it is better than the merchandise of silver, and the gain thereof than fine gold. She is more precious than rubies…. Length of days is in her right hand; and in her left hand riches and honour. Her ways are ways of pleasantness, and all her paths are peace. She is a tree of life to them that lay hold upon her: and happy is every one that retaineth her (Proverbs 3:13-18).

Every born-again believer has the wisdom of God residing on the inside of him. It is the same wisdom that God used when He created the universe. It is the same wisdom that Solomon used. It is ours because we are in Christ and He is in us. In Him are hid all the treasures of wisdom and knowledge (Colossians 2:3). He has been made unto us wisdom (1 Corinthians 1:30). He is The Word (John 1:1) and The Word is God's wisdom.

To utilize the wisdom of God we must first draw it out of our spirits and get it operating in our minds. The process can be likened to a well of water (Proverbs 20:5). Your conscious mind—your soul—is the top of the water, the surface. The deep water is your spirit. It is in contact with God because He is in there. Your spirit thinks the way He thinks. It has the mind of Christ (1 Corinthians 2:16). All that resides in your spirit is of God.

> *Every born-again believer has the wisdom of God residing on the inside of him.*

Water is drawn from a well by a bucket. Praying in tongues is our spiritual bucket with which we draw up God's wisdom. "For he that speaketh in an unknown tongue speaketh not unto men, but unto God: for no man understandeth him; howbeit in the spirit he speaketh mysteries" (1 Corinthians 14:2). When we pray in unknown tongues we are praying pure, uncompromised Word.

But the mind should not remain unfruitful. "Wherefore let him that speaketh in an unknown tongue pray that he may interpret" (1 Corinthians 14:13). When we know what the Spirit prayed through us to God, we can benefit from the wisdom that is there to guide us. Our minds will be renewed to the wisdom of God by the Holy Spirit, our teacher.

You will know it is of
the Spirit because He will show
you how to succeed. He will never
tell you that you can't do something
or show you that you will fail.
God's wisdom always brings total
prosperity: spirit, soul and body.

CD 4 Outlined

I. Wisdom is the ability to use knowledge
   A. God's Word is wisdom
      1. Prosperity is found in The Word

II. Jesus preached total prosperity

III. Solomon—a man of great wisdom
   A. Wisdom brought him wealth
   B. Key to success

IV. Believers must have the wisdom of God on the inside of them
   A. Jesus has been made unto us wisdom

V. Must utilize God's wisdom
   A. Draw it out of our spirits—deep water from the well
      1. Praying in tongues—spiritual bucket
   B. Operating in the conscious mind (soul)—surface water
      1. Interpreting tongues—mind fruitful and renewed to God's wisdom

IV. The Holy Spirit will always build and edify

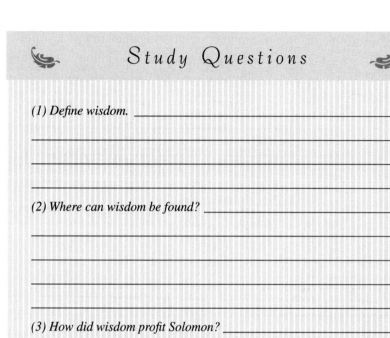

Study Questions

(1) Define wisdom. _____

_____

_____

_____

(2) Where can wisdom be found? _____

_____

_____

_____

_____

(3) How did wisdom profit Solomon? _____

_____

_____

_____

_____

(4) Why does every born-again believer have the wisdom of God on the inside of him? _____

_____

_____

_____

(5) How can wisdom be utilized? _____

_____

_____

_____

Study Notes

"The words of a man's mouth are as deep waters,
and the wellspring of wisdom as a flowing brook."
Proverbs 18:4

5

"Only be thou strong
and very courageous, that thou
mayest observe to do according
to all the law, which Moses my
servant commanded thee: turn
not from it to the right hand
or to the left, that
thou mayest prosper
whithersoever thou goest."

Joshua 1:7

CD FIVE
Prosperity in Abundance

Poverty No Longer Has Any Power

Stand on Your Redemption

Poverty is a curse. Although Jesus redeemed us from the curse, we must act on our redemption to benefit from its blessings.

Jairus came to Jesus on behalf of his daughter. He asked that Jesus come and lay hands on her and Jesus followed him. On the way, the woman with the issue of blood stopped Jesus when she touched His garment (Mark 5:22-43). Both people made a decision to make a demand on The Word and both received physical prosperity in abundance.

God has promised to meet our needs according to His riches in glory by Christ Jesus. It is His desire that we prosper and be in health (3 John 2). His prosperity is in His Word. Meditation in The Word of God will build an image on the inside of us that causes us to see ourselves as prosperous. Then, acting on The Word will bring the manifestation of that which we desire. The result will be a *prosperous and successful life.* This is what God gave to Joshua at a time when he needed instruction and guidance the most (Joshua 1:8).

> *We must act on our redemption to benefit from its blessings.*

The chastisement of our peace was upon Jesus. We are redeemed from worry and care. We have the privilege of rolling all our anxieties over on Him. Poverty is no longer our lord because Satan is no longer our lord. Jesus stripped him of his authority. If it had not been God's will for us to be blessed, He would never have sent Jesus to purchase our freedom.

> His
>
> prosperity
>
> is in
>
> His Word.

Jesus preached an entire sermon in Matthew 6 about the laws of prosperity. He said that we could lay up treasures in heaven where neither moth nor rust corrupts and thieves do not break through nor steal.

When you invest in God's work and do the things of God, you are laying up treasure that you can withdraw by faith whenever you need it. You do not have to wait, it is accessible now. God is your source and prosperity is in His Word.

$\mathcal{C}\mathcal{D}$ 5 $\mathcal{O}utlined$

I. Poverty is a curse
  A. We are delivered by acting on our redemption

II. Man is the deciding factor
  A. Jairus made a decision
  B. Woman with the issue of blood made a decision

III. Formula God gave Joshua for prosperity and success
  A. Meditate The Word
    1. Forms an inner image of success
  B. Talk The Word
  C. Act on The Word

IV. Worry is meditation on the world's way
  A. The chastisement of our peace was upon Jesus

V. Jesus preached the laws of prosperity (Matthew 6)
  A. Giving lays up treasure in heaven that you can draw
    from now, by faith

Study Questions

(1) How do we activate our redemption? _____

_____

_____

_____

_____

(2) Why did Jairus and the woman with the issue of blood receive?

_____

_____

_____

_____

(3) How do you live a prosperous and successful life? _____

_____

_____

_____

(4) Why is worry detrimental to prosperity? _____

_____

_____

_____

_____

(5) How do you lay up treasures in heaven? _____

_____

_____

_____

_____

Study Notes

"...*Verily I say unto you, There is no man that hath left house, or brethren, or sisters, or father, or mother, or wife, or children, or lands, for my sake, and the gospel's, but he shall receive an hundredfold now in this time...and in the world to come eternal life.*"
Mark 10:29-30

6

"*Lay up for yourselves treasures in heaven, where neither moth nor rust doth corrupt, and where thieves do not break through nor steal: For where your treasure is, there will your heart be also.*"

Matthew 6:20-21

CD SIX

Depositing and Withdrawing

Every Time You Act on The
Word in the Area of Prosperity,
You Have Certain Rights and
Privileges in Which Heaven
Will Back You

Be Ready to Distribute

The Word's definition of prosperity is the ability to call on heaven's power to meet a man's need—spirit, soul, body, financially and socially. When God is involved in a man's affairs, there is no limit to what can be done.

Jesus said, "If ye continue in my word, then are ye my disciples indeed; And ye shall know the truth, and the truth shall make you free" (John 8:31-32). The word *continue* is the same word for "meditate" in Joshua 1:8. If you meditate in the Word of God you will know the truth and that truth will make you free. A free man is a man who lives in prosperity—spirit, soul, body, financially and socially. He is a man who lives in The Word.

> *The Word's definition of prosperity is the ability to call on heaven's power to meet a man's need.*

Being financially prosperous does not necessarily mean just money. God can prosper you with things like clothes, cars, material things, etc. You can give things other than money and lay up for yourself treasures in heaven. They are credited to your heavenly bank account but you do not have to wait until you get to heaven to make withdrawals. When a need arises, you can make a withdrawal on your account. "Seek ye first the kingdom of God, and his righteousness; and all these things shall be added unto you" (Matthew 6:33). When you seek God and His Word, all these things will be added to you. And everything will be in its proper perspective. Almighty God is your supreme provider. He meets all your need according to His riches in glory by Christ Jesus.

Abram, a man of great wealth, refused the spoils of battle that the king of Sodom offered. He said, "I will not take from a thread even to a shoelatchet, and that I will not take any thing that is thine, lest thou shouldest say, I have made Abram rich" (Genesis 14:23). He depended on God and he was abundantly blessed.

God never changes. He gives us richly all things to enjoy. He has never condemned a man for possessing great wealth. He has, however, cautioned against being high-minded and *trusting* in riches (1 Timothy 6:17).

Almighty God is your supreme provider.

Commit to believe The Word in this area. When Satan comes immediately to try to stop you or steal The Word from you concerning prosperity, remember, he is a defeated foe. He knows that God's men will use their finances to further the gospel. God is a giver and His will for man is to be a giver.

There are four areas of giving that
will lay up treasures in heaven.
One way is giving as a praise to God.
A group of Navajo Indians brought
polished rocks, and anything else
they could find, to the Lord as an
offering of praise. They did not wait
until they had prospered to give.
As a result, God blessed them and their
church. The intent of their heart was the
determining factor of their prosperity.

CD 6 Outlined

I. The Word's definition of prosperity

II. Prosperity is in The Word
   A. The truth will make you free (John 8:31-32)
      1. A free man is a prosperous man

III. Seek first the kingdom of God and all these things will
   be added unto you (Matthew 6:33)

IV. God blesses us richly in order to further the gospel

V. Giving is not the only way to lay up treasure in heaven
   A. One way is as a praise to God

Study Questions

(1) What is The Word's definition of prosperity? _____

_____

_____

_____

(2) What does the word **continue** *in John 8:31 mean?* _____

_____

_____

_____

_____

(3) Name some ways that God can prosper you and how you can give other than with money. _____

_____

_____

_____

(4) Why does God give men the power to get wealth? _____

_____

_____

_____

(5) Name one area of giving that lays up treasure in heaven. _____

_____

_____

_____

_____

Study Notes

"...*If ye continue in my word, then are ye my disciples indeed; and ye shall know the truth, and the truth shall make you free.*"
John 8:31-32

7

"And thou shalt speak
and say.... And now,
behold, I have brought the
firstfruits of the land,
which thou, O Lord, hast
given me. And thou shalt
set it before the Lord thy
God, and worship before
the Lord thy God."

Deuteronomy 26:5, 10

CD SEVEN
Depositing and Withdrawing
(continued)

God Is Always Planning More Prosperity for You— Not Less

Faith—The Activity of Giving *and* Receiving

Investing in the gospel is another way to lay up for yourself treasure in heaven. Jesus told the rich young ruler that he would have treasure in heaven if he would sell what he had and give to the poor (Mark 10:21).

The rich young ruler was grieved. His faith was not in God's ability or he would have immediately heeded the words of Jesus. Had he done so, the scripture which says, "He that hath pity upon the poor lendeth unto the Lord; and that which he hath given will he pay him again," would have been manifest in his life (Proverbs 19:17). It was God who had blessed him financially but his trust was in his riches. He looked to them as his source. This is why Jesus said, "How hardly shall they that have riches enter into the kingdom of God" (Mark 10:23).

> *Investing in the gospel is a way to lay up for yourself treasure in heaven.*

Tithing is still another way to lay up treasure in heaven. Many people today do not consider tithing a New Testament principle. Hebrews 7:8 states: "And here men that die receive tithes; but there he receiveth them, of whom it is witnessed that he liveth." Jesus is receiving tithes in heaven.

Deuteronomy 26 outlines how to tithe. It was instituted by God for the children of Israel so they could be blessed financially.

Verse 1: "And it shall be, when thou art come in unto the land which the Lord thy God giveth thee for an inheritance, and possessest it, and dwellest therein...." We have come into the land which the Lord gave us. We have been delivered from the power of darkness and have been translated into the kingdom of God (Colossians 1:13). We are possessors of that land and we are living in it now.

> *We have come into the land which the Lord gave us.*

Verses 2-3: "That thou shalt take of the first of all the fruit of the earth... and shalt go unto the place which the Lord thy God shall choose to place his name there. And thou shalt go unto the priest that shall be in those days, and say unto him...." We are in Christ. The Body of Christ, the Church, is called by His Name. We are to take our tithe—10 percent of the gross—to the church, pastor, evangelist, teacher, etc. where Jesus tells us. We are tithing to Him, not a man. He is the High Priest of our profession (Hebrews 3:1). He is the High Priest of the tithe.

Verses 5-10 tell what the Israelites professed. They were giving Him praise and thanksgiving for His deliverance and His blessings. ◈

Tithing is twofold—giving and receiving. Decide the amount you need to increase your standard of living by and believe God for the return to meet that standard. He said, "Bring ye all the tithes into the storehouse, that there may be meat in mine house, and prove me now herewith, saith the Lord of hosts, if I will not open you the windows of heaven, and pour you out a blessing, that there shall not be room enough to receive it" (Malachi 3:10).

CD 7 Outlined

I. Investing in the gospel is one area of giving that lays up treasure in heaven
  A. Example: The rich young ruler (Mark 10:17-31)
    1. Trusted in riches more than God
    2. He missed
      a. Possible discipleship
      b. Treasure in heaven
      c. Financial blessing

II. Tithing is still another way to lay up treasure in heaven
  A. New Testament principle
    1. Jesus lives and receives tithes in heaven

III. Outline of tithing (Deuteronomy 26)
  A. We possess our inheritance—kingdom
  B. Take the first fruit—10 percent of the gross
    1. Jesus instructs us where to put it
  C. We profess to Jesus our High Priest
    1. Thank and praise Him for blessings
    2. Never should words be stout against Him

IV. Tithing is twofold—giving and receiving by faith

V. Tithing is the only area of faith in which you can prove God
  A. Bring meat into My storehouse—give
  B. Pour you out a blessing—receive

Study Questions

(1) What did the rich young ruler miss by not heeding the words of Jesus? _____

_____

_____

_____

(2) Why is tithing a New Testament as well as an Old Testament principle?

_____

_____

_____

_____

_____

(3) Why is the tithe to Jesus and not to men? _____

_____

_____

_____

_____

(4) What part do words play in tithing? _____

_____

_____

_____

(5) Tithing is a twofold principle. It is _____

and _____.

Study Notes

"...I assure you, most solemnly I tell you, that My Father will grant you whatever you ask in My Name [as presenting all that I AM]."
John 16:23, The Amplified Bible

8

"And God blessed
them and said to them,
Be fruitful, multiply,
and fill the earth, and
subdue it [using all its
vast resources in the
service of God
and man]...."

Genesis 1:28, The Amplified Bible

CD EIGHT
Divine Prosperity
by Gloria Copeland

You Can Depend
on The Word of God—
It Never Fails!

The Decision Is Up to You

Act on The Word because you want to please the Father.
Seek first the kingdom of God and as a result, all the things you
desire will be added to you. That's
the way the laws of prosperity work.
It's a built-in protection. It would be
a dangerous situation if it were the
other way around. Third John 2 says
you'll prosper *as* your soul prospers.
You won't get it any other way. You
can't get it out of balance. You'll get
financial prosperity to the degree that
your soul prospers.

> *You'll get financial prosperity to the degree that your soul prospers.*

Second Corinthians 9:8 says,
"And God is able to make all grace (every favor and earthly
blessing) come to you in abundance, so that you may always
and under all circumstances and whatever the need be self-
sufficient [possessing enough to require no aid or support and
furnished in abundance for every good work and charitable
donation]" *(The Amplified Bible).*

God is able! You don't have to waver. You can believe God
for something and never go back on it. You don't have to go
back and forth. Believe God for something, and stay with it.
Don't look to natural things—to your job or natural resources.
Take your confidence in the fact that He is able, that He can get
the job done.

The decision is up to you. Isaiah 1:19 says, "If ye be willing
and obedient, ye shall eat the good of the land." Willing has
become a passive word in this age. "Well, I'm willing (ready) to
go to this place." The *willing* used in this scripture involves a
decision. It is an action word. When you say, "I am willing to
live in divine health," it doesn't mean that if somebody slaps it

on you, you'll live in it. Instead, you've made up your mind, you've made the decision, you *will* live in health. You are not willing to be sick. Make a quality decision that you *will* live in prosperity.

God gave man dominion and authority over all of the earth's vast resources (Genesis 1:28, *The Amplified Bible*). Everything we see, either in raw or finished form, is a resource taken from the earth. After His resurrection, Jesus reinstated man with the same authority that Adam had from the beginning. Every need man would ever have is under this dominion. ༺༄

Every time thoughts of defeat and discouragement come, remember The Word. If you stand on The Word, knowing what belongs to you, Satan cannot be successful against you. He has no authority, and he has to flee.

CD 8 Outlined

I. Seek first the kingdom
   A. The result—things desired will be added
   B. Built-in protection, can't get out of balance

II. Use The Word to maintain your faith (2 Corinthians 9:8)
   A. Don't look to the natural
   B. God can get the job done

III. Jesus redeemed you from poverty the same way He
   did from sickness

IV. Make the decision that you *will* live in prosperity

V. We have authority over all the earth's vast resources
   A. Money is a resource of the earth

Study Questions

(1) What is the result of seeking first the kingdom of God? _____

_____

_____

_____

_____

(2) To what degree will you prosper? _____

_____

_____

_____

_____

(3) How can you know that God will prosper you? _____

_____

_____

_____

_____

(4) Is poverty under the curse? _____

_____

_____

_____

(5) Why does Satan have to flee when you stand on The Word? _____

_____

_____

_____

_____

Study Notes

"Oh, that you had hearkened to My commandments! Then your peace and prosperity would have been like a flowing river, and your righteousness...like the [abundant] waves of the sea."
Isaiah 48:18, The Amplified Bible

Prayer for Salvation and Baptism in the Holy Spirit

Heavenly Father, I come to You in the Name of Jesus. Your Word says, "Whosoever shall call on the name of the Lord shall be saved" (Acts 2:21). I am calling on You. I pray and ask Jesus to come into my heart and be Lord over my life according to Romans 10:9-10: "If thou shalt confess with thy mouth the Lord Jesus, and shalt believe in thine heart that God hath raised him from the dead, thou shalt be saved. For with the heart man believeth unto righteousness; and with the mouth confession is made unto salvation." I do that now. I confess that Jesus is Lord, and I believe in my heart that God raised Him from the dead. I repent of sin. I renounce it. I renounce the devil and everything he stands for. Jesus is my Lord.

I am now reborn! I am a Christian—a child of Almighty God! I am saved! You also said in Your Word, "If ye then, being evil, know how to give good gifts unto your children: HOW MUCH MORE shall your heavenly Father give the Holy Spirit to them that ask him?" (Luke 11:13). I'm also asking You to fill me with the Holy Spirit. Holy Spirit, rise up within me as I praise God. I fully expect to speak with other tongues as You give me the utterance (Acts 2:4). In Jesus' Name. Amen!

Begin to praise God for filling you with the Holy Spirit. Speak those words and syllables you receive—not in your own language, but the language given to you by the Holy Spirit. You have to use your own voice. God will not force you to speak. Don't be concerned with how it sounds. It is a heavenly language!

Continue with the blessing God has given you and pray in the spirit every day.

You are a born-again, Spirit-filled believer. You'll never be the same!

Find a good church that boldly preaches God's Word and obeys it. Become part of a church family who will love and care for you as you love and care for them.

We need to be connected to each other. It increases our strength in God. It's God's plan for us.

Make it a habit to watch the Believer's Voice of Victory Network and become a doer of the Word, who is blessed in his doing (James 1:22-25).

About the Authors

Kenneth and Gloria Copeland are the best-selling authors of more than 60 books. They have also co-authored numerous books including *Family Promises,* the *LifeLine* series and *From Faith to Faith—A Daily Guide to Victory.* As founders of Kenneth Copeland Ministries in Fort Worth, Texas, Kenneth and Gloria have been circling the globe with the uncompromised Word of God since 1967, preaching and teaching a lifestyle of victory for every Christian.

Their daily and Sunday *Believer's Voice of Victory* television broadcasts now air on more than 500 stations around the world, and the *Believer's Voice of Victory* magazine is distributed to nearly 600,000 believers worldwide. Kenneth Copeland Ministries' international prison ministry reaches more than 20,000 new inmates every year and receives more than 20,000 pieces of correspondence each month. Their teaching materials can also be found on the World Wide Web. With offices and staff in the United States, Canada, England, Australia, South Africa, Ukraine and Singapore, Kenneth and Gloria's teaching materials—books, magazines, audios and videos—have been translated into at least 26 languages to reach the world with the love of God.

When The LORD first spoke to Kenneth and Gloria Copeland about starting the *Believer's Voice of Victory* magazine...

He said: *This is your seed. Give it to everyone who ever responds to your ministry, and don't ever allow anyone to pay for a subscription!*

For more than 40 years, it has been the joy of Kenneth Copeland Ministries to bring the good news to believers. Readers enjoy teaching from ministers who write from lives of living contact with God, and testimonies from believers experiencing victory through God's WORD in their everyday lives.

Today, the *BVOV* magazine is mailed monthly, bringing encouragement and blessing to believers around the world. Many even use it as a ministry tool, passing it on to others who desire to know Jesus and grow in their faith!

Request your FREE subscription to the *Believer's Voice of Victory* magazine today!

Go to **freevictory.com** to subscribe online, or call us at **1-800-600-7395** (U.S. only) or **+1-817-852-6000**.

We're Here for You!®

Your growth in God's WORD and victory in Jesus are at the very center of our hearts. In every way God has equipped us, we will help you deal with the issues facing you, so you can be the **victorious overcomer** He has planned for you to be.

The mission of Kenneth Copeland Ministries is about all of us growing and going together. Our prayer is that you will take full advantage of all The LORD has given us to share with you.

Wherever you are in the world, you can watch the *Believer's Voice of Victory* broadcast on television (check your local listings), the Internet at kcm.org or on our digital Roku channel.

Our website, **kcm.org,** gives you access to every resource we've developed for your victory. And, you can find contact information for our international offices in Africa, Asia, Australia, Canada, Europe, Ukraine and our headquarters in the United States.

Each office is staffed with devoted men and women, ready to serve and pray with you. You can contact the worldwide office nearest you for assistance, and you can call us for prayer at our U.S. number, +1-817-852-6000, 24 hours every day!

We encourage you to connect with us often and let us be part of your everyday walk of faith!

Jesus Is LORD!

Kenneth & Gloria Copeland

Kenneth and Gloria Copeland